NICK'S HAMBURGER SHOP

By Chuck Cecil

Nick's Hamburger Shop
Copyright © 2007 by
Chuck Cecil

ISBN: 978-1-57579-361-0

Library of Congress Control Number: 2007930556

Printed in the United States of America

PINE HILL PRESS
4000 West 57th Street
Sioux Falls, SD 57106

To Nickburger fans everywhere
(including the two I believe are living on Mars).

- Chuck Cecil

Saturday, Oct. 18, 1947, was a red letter day in Brookings.

It even ranked above the October arrival of the first-ever helicopter in town. It raised a swirling cloud of dust when it set down at the ball field near Hillcrest Park, and hundreds of curious, interested citizens and wide-eyed Brookings youngsters turned out to see their first flying "egg beater," as the *Brookings Register* reported.

That wasn't the only big cloud of dust raised in Brookings that October. There was plenty of it the week before, too. It was stirred up by the more than 35,000 homecoming well-wishers lining the Hobo Day parade route through downtown Brookings, and later that day, in a hard-hitting Hobo Day football game at State Field.

Everything was properly and joyously aligned that historic day. South Dakota State College, which had been nearly devoid of male students during the war years 1941 to 1945, was recovering from the reduced enrollment and the drastic measures necessary during the world's second war.

Now it was finally over. Former service men and women were back in class at the university (then still a college), and other veterans were home from far-off fox holes and battle stations on every continent and ocean. A bright future was before them as the cloud of death and destruction slowly drifted off to history's ash pot.

Normalcy was returning. Gasoline, oil, tires, and vehicles were no longer rationed. Leisure time and travel were possible again. For the first time since 1942, people were able to come to Brookings to join in the state's biggest homecoming event. And they came in record-setting droves.

After the morning parade, and before and after the Hobo Day football game at State Field, they all looked for a place to eat. The town's few restaurants were packed, as was Nick's Hamburger Shop. It was Nick's—a Brookings icon even then—that most of them remembered.

So the little shop's fare was flying out of the cooking tank that day. A constant stream of customers stopped in. It would be a record day at Nick's. Enough of the small, inexpensive but delicious hamburgers were sold that Oct. 18, 1947, that if laid out bun to bun, they would stretch the entire length of the three-block parade route through downtown Brookings.

Put another way, if all the Nickburgers eaten that Hobo Day were stacked one atop the other, the pile would reach well beyond the height of the 165-foot Coughlin Campanile, which coincidentally, had been completed in the same year, 1929, that the Harold Niklason family brought their unique hamburger shop to Brookings.

The 1947 Hobo Day serving of ten-cent Nickburgers numbered 4,450. It is a record that remains today. No wonder.

Appetites for fun, frivolity, and food were at a zenith in 1947, thirty-five years after the first Hobo Day in 1912. If there ever was a time to eat, drink, and be merry, this was it. The war was over. Veterans, lean from their mostly field diet of C-rations, had money in their pockets and fond memories of their former collegiate days on their minds.

As Harold and Gladys Niklason were building their new business in town in 1929, the Coughlin Campanile was going up on the college campus. Both the Campanile and Nick's Hamburger Shop opened on the same day in 1929.

True, there had been a Hobo Day of sorts in 1946 after the war ended on August 14, 1945. But that one came during the difficult conversion from war time to peace time. Many GI's, sailors, and airmen were still on duty or awaiting a slow boat back to the states. Finally, in 1947, the men and women were back, and it was business as usual. All was well. It was really the first homecoming after the war with the nation having finally returned to a more relaxed, happier, peace-time cadence.

Harold Niklason Jr. was back home, too. He'd spent most of the war in the Army Engineers sweating it out in the South Pacific and Philippines. A few months after he was honorably discharged and back in Brookings, he worked out a deal with his folks to buy the hamburger shop on the busy Brookings corner.

The war years had been difficult for everyone, including the Niklason family and their hamburger shop. Because of rationing, it had been open only three days a week. Now, with the family back together, it was a welcome chore for Harold Jr. and his parents Harold and Gladys to spend that entire 1947 Hobo Day on their feet and working feverishly trying to keep up with the constant flow of customers into the little shop at the corner of Fifth Street and Main Avenue. And while they worked, they were also enjoying the camaraderie of old friendships with former customers, friends, and buddies returning for the homecoming and the big game.

"It was the biggest day we ever had," remembered Harold Jr. years later. "The next Hobo Day, in 1948, we came close, serving 4,350 hamburgers."

But Hobo Day 1947 took the cake.

Brookings Police Chief Jim Connelly estimated the crowd lining the morning parade route at 35,000. People were standing four and five deep along most of the eighteen-block route from the campus to Main Avenue. The parade had more than eighty units, with displays—as usual—ranging from the spectacular to the absurd. Many visiting high school bands and the famed Jackrabbit Marching Band were interspersed among the floats and stunt cars, all making it the largest Hobo Day parade since the unique event was started in 1912. The cavalcade passed by Nick's Hamburger Shop for a full ninety minutes.

Guests of Brookings and the college that day included Governor and Mrs. George Mickelson and Congressman and Mrs. Karl Mundt. Lieutenant Governor and Mrs. S. K. Grigsby attended, as did University of South Dakota President I. D. Weeks and his wife. All seven members of the

Board of Regents were at the afternoon football game along with an estimated 10,500 others.

As the parade passed by, war hero, flying ace, and Medal of Honor recipient Joe Foss, who would one day be South Dakota's governor, was briefing several of his fellow fighter pilots fifty miles away in Sioux Falls as they prepared for a thrilling, noisy South Dakota Air National Guard

A Hobo Day float in the 1950s

fighter plane fly-by just before kickoff of the South Dakota State College-University of South Dakota football game.

The night before the game, during the college's beard judging contest, Jim Dornbush, a civil engineering student who later earned his doctorate degree and would return and devote his entire career to teaching in the College of Engineering, was selected winner of the longest beard competition at Sylvan Outdoor Theater on campus. The next day, Hobo Day, he was picked "king of hoboes" during halftime of the football game. It was a double honor for the Pollock native.

After the parade, Nick's suddenly became a very busy place as the first several hundred of the day's total of 4,450 hamburgers were sold. The call for more Nickburgers continued through the day, then abated somewhat during the afternoon game, which the Jackrabbits lost 26-8. Fans mourned the loss of the Little Brown Jug, a symbol of the contest, which was joyously carried onto the bus with the Coyotes team and taken to Vermillion to await the next year's contest.

Despite the disappointing loss on the playing field, there was peace in the world, and plenty of Nickburgers were left for the continued celebrating and feasting that continued until closing time at 10 p.m. that beautiful Saturday.

Nick's Hamburger Shop had been "wowing" Jackrabbit fans and others in Brookings and the area for eighteen years before that record-breaking day in 1947.

It was 1929 when the shop first fired up its stove, which burned what was referred to then as "white gasoline" for fuel. Nick's at that time was located in a small, nondescript shop across the street and west from its present home. That space is now the well-appointed conference room for Steen Bookkeeping. But back then it wasn't much at all except a place where you could buy good hamburgers for a nickel. Little did anyone know that the shop would be around for decades and become an icon in Brookings and the area. Only Rude's Home Furnishings several blocks down the street would earn more longevity for a Brookings business.

Since 1929, millions of Nickburgers have been enjoyed by probably hundreds of thousands of people. The shop is a magnet that brings generations together. Everyone who has been a Nickburger admirer through the decades has developed an emotional attachment to the place and to the little hamburgers that are still offered at bargain prices.

The shop's almost instant success in Brookings surprised even the Niklasons. They had decided to locate in Brookings but were unsure if their stay would be permanent. In fact, they left their youngest daughter at home with relatives in Spencer, Iowa, until they knew that Brookings was the town for them.

Many of their friends in the Spencer area didn't give them much of a chance. "They thought we'd be broke in a few weeks," remembered Harold Jr., who was nine when the family arrived in Brookings.

The future of a hamburger shop in Brookings was also questioned by Brookings folks. Part of the deal when the Niklasons rented the space behind the J. C. Penney Store from Iver Dybdahl, a local car dealer, was that Dybdahl would hire someone to paint the place.

Dybdahl told the painter not to bother with the ceiling. "I told him that the new owners would probably go broke in thirty days and leave," a smiling Dybdahl confided to a *Brookings Register* reporter years later.

Despite predictions of failure, and during the nation's worst economic depression, especially devastating in farm country that had to endure months of crushing heat and no rainfall, Harold and Gladys, with young Harold Jr. in tow, hooked the back legs of an old stove over the car's rear bumper, lashed it solid with rope, and departed on their uncertain, arduous journey to Brookings. Consideration of that destination had come about because of an off-the-cuff remark by one of Niklason's contacts during an earlier, exploratory trip to the Brookings-Madison area seeking a possible site for their hamburger shop.

Harold and Gladys seemed to favor a Madison location. It appeared to be a better place for their little business. Then someone allowed as how they thought that Madison was more of a drinking town than Brookings. That was all Gladys needed to hear. She immediately decided Brookings would be the location for their new business. "They actually liked the Madison area better," remembered Harold Jr.

Consideration of the Brookings area in the first place was also by happenstance. Harold and Gladys knew of the success Gladys' father Tom Swezey had after buying a small hamburger shop in Spencer. After their marriage, they were working in the shop when a man from Brookings dropped in. He enjoyed his hamburgers and commented to Harold and Gladys that his hometown of Brookings, South Dakota, should have something like the Spencer shop.

At the time, many of Tom Swezey's relatives and friends were opening similar shops in nearby towns. Eventually over seventy restaurants and hamburger shops had been started all over the nation by Swezey's friends and relatives using the tank fry method that Swezey perfected.

Swezey's success came in the era of the growth of the White Castle hamburger chain. It was founded in 1921 in Wichita, Kansas, by Billy Ingram and a cook, Walter Anderson. At the time, Americans were hesitant to eat ground beef after Upton Sinclair's 1906 novel, *The Jungle*, had publicized the poor sanitation practices of the meat packing industry. Incidentally, Brookings residents referred to its business district as Main Street until Sinclair's *Main Street* novel gave main streets everywhere a bad name. After the book was published, city fathers decided that Brookings should comply with the rest of the city's avenues oriented north and south, and changed its downtown drag to Main Avenue.

Billy Ingram and Walter Anderson set out to change the public's perception of the hamburger.

They constructed small buildings with hygienically white exteriors and stainless steel fixtures and outfitted their employees with spotless uniforms. Their hamburgers were formed into balls by machine, eighteen to a pound, and the balls were fried with onions on a hot grill, not placed in a fry tank "a cappella" as was Swezey's method.

The so-called tank fry method would gradually succumb to the faster, easier method of fried hamburgers employed in most of the fast food purveyors of today. In fact, the only remaining Tom Swezey establishment left is Nick's Hamburger Shop in Brookings, S.D. There have been some wanna-be imitations of the Nick's shop over the years, but most have not survived. Nick's Hamburger Shop in Brookings remains a unique place for its one-of-a-kind gastronomical treat.

Harold and Gladys Niklason's evolving business plan in Brookings mirrored somewhat the White Castle approach: white building, white interior, white uniforms and caps, and stainless steel fixtures. It was all very simple and straightforward: sell as many hamburgers as you could as cheaply as you could, and reduce the overhead expense as much as possible by limiting traditional restaurant accoutrements such as dishes and silverware to as few as possible. Above all, avoid the temptation to expand the menu. It needed to be simple and with no frills, start to finish. Finally, then as now, the Nickburger method included polite, friendly cooks and helpful waiters and waitresses.

"When we first started in Brookings we didn't even have a cash register," Harold Jr. remembered. "We used a tin cupcake pan." The first shop was also void of any expensive equipment other than the stove carted up from Spencer on which sat the fry tank, as it was known, filled with its bubbling oil.

There were few dishes to wash, dry, store, and break, and no silverware to speak of except a few forks added to the inventory after the Niklasons added pie to the menu. A few lonely spoons joined the Nickburger eatery platoon to stir sugar into the coffee as some customers preferred. Hamburgers were and still are served up on small squares of special non-absorbent paper set out on the counter in front of the customer, facilitating easy and rapid clean up.

In an early-day photograph of Harold F. Niklason standing outside his shop at 315 Fifth Street next to the pool hall that is now Steen's Bookkeeping, the display window sign behind him urges customers to "buy 'em by the sack." That slogan remains the catch phrase today. Another window message behind Niklason advertises five cent hamburgers and "good coffee." That photograph was probably taken in about 1930 to send home to the folks back in Spencer, Iowa.

Shortly after opening the doors in 1929, Harold Niklason posed outside his new business across graveled Fifth Street from the present location. Note the "ladies welcome" sign.

In that old photograph, incidentally, just west across the alley to Harold's right, was the town's old Grand Army of the Republic (GAR) post home (311 Fifth Street). It was built by local Civil War veterans in 1884 after they settled in Brookings in the 1870s and 1880s. Many town meetings, political rallies, and grand banquets were held in that hall over the years, including a joyous welcome home ceremony and banquet for Brookings County young men returning from the Spanish-American war battles in the Philippines in 1899. The GAR Hall gradually fell into disrepair as the aging veterans died, and the old building was moved to a site at 126 Medary Avenue next to the railroad tracks. It became the Odd Fellows Hall and was razed in about 2000 to make room for a new facility built for storage and as the home of Virg Anderson's Car Care, Tire and Alignment Shop.

When Harold and Gladys Niklason opened in Brookings in 1929, their next door neighbor on Fifth Street was this Grand Army of the Republic (GAR) Hall, built in the 1880s by Civil War veterans. It was later moved to a site just south of the railroad tracks on Medary Ave. and became the Odd fellows Hall. That was later razed and the Odd fellow Rental unit was built by Paul Prussman. Virg Anderson's car service center is also now at this site.

Although the star of the menu at Nick's was the little hamburger, it wasn't the only popular item for sale. Coffee often drew as many raves from diners. Harold and Gladys had packed several one-pound cans of Folgers Coffee in their Chevrolet when they left Spencer for Brookings. "We were the first ones in Brookings to serve Folgers Coffee," son Harold Jr. remembered. "You couldn't buy Folgers coffee here until two years after we opened our shop."

Part of the secret to the good coffee, Harold Jr. claimed, was that his mother believed Brookings city tap water at that time did not enhance the taste of Folgers. She arranged to get water for their coffee from a nearby well in the backyard of a local homeowner. It was Harold Jr.'s daily job to draw enough water from the well each morning for the day's supply of coffee.

Another task for young Niklason was to pull his little red wagon to the Texaco Station a block away at the corner of Main Avenue and Sixth Street where Moriarty's Rental Office is today. The attendant at the station would fill the five-gallon gas can in the wagon with white gas for the shop's stove.

The first day of business for what was then just "The Hamburger Shop" was on Hobo Day, Nov. 2, 1929. Harold and his parents and an employee, Elsie Albrecht, all donned white caps, tied on white aprons, and went to work. The legend of the famous Nickburger has been growing since.

Business wasn't exacting booming on that first day for The Hamburger Shop. Harold Jr. remembered that it was just "okay." He recalled that the business did get a boost from Lou Lemert, manager of the J. C. Penney store nearby, now Robb

Rasmussen's Sioux River Bicycles and Fitness store. Lemert told his employees to have their lunch on him at the new shop behind his store. With that added customer count, the makeshift tin cupcake pan cash register was heavier at the end of the day, and Harold and Gladys sensed that their stay in Brookings would be longer than their families back in Spencer had assumed. And Mr. Dybdahl pondered having the shop's ceiling painted.

Those early-day Nickburgers were small compared to today's fare. The first servings from the Niklason shop weighed about an ounce and were small enough to be served on a freshly baked bun that was actually a dinner roll. For several decades, Nickburgers have been at about two ounces, and part of their appeal is that they are served in delicious buns baked fresh daily following Niklason's old family recipe.

After that Hobo Day grand opening in 1929, word of the nickel hamburger spread. The new business prospered and became one of the most popular eating establishments on that dusty Brookings side street during the early years of the Great Depression, when eating out for most people wasn't a daily or even weekly treat.

So successful was the business that on February 1, 1933, Gladys and Harold moved it to 427

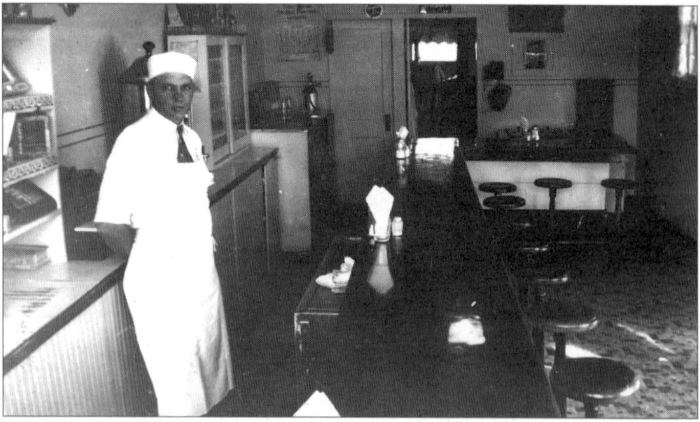

This photo was taken in 1933 shortly after the Niklasons moved into the location that is still Nick's Hamburger Shop.

Main Avenue, on the corner where it has been since. Because their inventory was not large (a stove, a few dishes, and the tin cupcake pan cash register), they made the move in an hour or so after they closed for the night at 10 p.m. on a chilly Tuesday, January 31, 1933.

At that time, there were 879 students attending State College. The high school announced it was adding solid geometry and botany as new second semester courses. The town was abuzz about the collapse of a portion of the second floor of the Montgomery-Ward store (now Skinner's Pub) from the weight of the new rolls of linoleum on display. And a block away from the Monkey-Ward store, as it was called, the Sexauer Elevator was handling the storage of eight hundred sacks of flour the Red Cross donated to the county to be distributed to those in need because of the economically depressed conditions.

The new location for the hamburger shop was a small stucco building with a pronounced Spanish or Mexican adobe influence. The building design may have been influenced by the growing popularity of the White Castle hamburger shops springing up throughout the Midwest. But the design was more likely because its Brookings builder, local carpenter Fred Carlson, had spent time in the building trades in California and had built many structures with a west coast touch.

Carlson, the great uncle of Jerry Danielson of rural Bruce and younger brother Dick Danielson of Brookings, had earlier constructed a unique Dutch windmill concession stand on south Sixth Street in the early 1920s. The windmill's four blades could actually turn. Carlson mounted lights on them which helped bring out the children for treats after the sun went down. The windmill was located at the corner of First

Avenue and Sixth Street near Carlson's cabinet shop. He later became an automobile mechanic in Brookings, and during the height of the Great Depression just before the war, he moved back to California. His building at the corner of Fifth Street and Main Avenue, of Mexican adobe or Spanish castle design, has changed little since that first day on February 1, 1933.

The building was twenty-five feet wide and forty feet long. It is still just twenty-five feet wide, but twenty or thirty feet have since been added to its length. The Hamburger Shop took up the north half of the building, which meant the shop's working counter, customer counter, stools, and standing space were squeezed into about twelve feet. The 480 square feet in the south half of the building has been home to a number of businesses through the years, including an insurance office, a draft beer bar, and a barber.

The very first business in the south side of the building was Red's Cigar Store and News Stand, which was opened in early 1933 by Julius Jacobson. He had been working down the street at Taylor's Corner for eleven years when

This car was stranded in mid-intersection in front of Nick's shop during a vicious 1963 blizzard. Note buildings to the left of Nick's, which were destroyed by fire in March 1985.

he decided to go into business for himself. In an announcement of his plans, he said he would carry the usual line of cigars, plus pipes, a variety of tobaccos, fountain service, candy bars, newspapers, and magazines.

Interestingly, Taylor's Corner where Jacobson worked became Logue's Corner in 1934 and then Ray's Corner in 1959. Ray's is now owned by Mike Fergen, younger brother of the current owner of the Nick's Hamburger Shop building.

During the early 1940 war years, the south half was a tiny, watch-fob-sized bar known as the "7-0 Club," so named because that's what its telephone number was. There's a wonderful old photograph of that 7-0 Club, with Jim Urquardt, owner-bartender, drawing draft beer for about twenty-five members of the famous State College "44 Kings." Urquardt later started Jim's Tap down the street, which is still open today. The photograph was taken on October 8, 1943. The exact date is known because earlier that day, the same cadre of collegians, all smartly attired in their newly-issued Army dress uniforms, had attended the wedding of a member of their distinguished

State College ROTC soldiers enjoy an afternoon beer at the 7-0 Club that during WW II was in the south half of the Nick's Hamburger Shop building. The only young man in this photo to lose his life in the war was Gene Ambur, who can be seen at far right center.

group, Tom Lyons, who married Shirley Graham, daughter of the Chicago & North Western Depot Railway Company depot agent in town.

The 44 Kings were ROTC students taken from classes and sent away for officers training, then returned to classes at State College to await assignments during WW II. It was and still is a close-knit corps of now aging veterans. They were nicknamed "Kings" because they had been army-trained and were officers earning a regular salary. They were treated like kings by the admiring coeds and others on campus.

That photograph shows the group enjoying a beer following the wedding ceremony at the First Baptist Church two blocks away on Fifth Street. All of the young men in the photograph later went off to war, serving in Europe as well as in the South Pacific. One of them was Lt. Sherwood O. Berg, who commanded a mortar platoon in

Europe and years later earned his doctorate degree, was Dean of Agriculture at the University of Minnesota, and in 1970 returned as the first State College graduate to serve as president of what is now South Dakota State University.

Only one of the young men in the photograph failed to return after the war. Handsome, blond Gene Ambur of Beresford was killed in action. He can be seen in the photograph, on page 32 of this book, happy and smiling with his compatriots during this impromptu celebration at the 7-0 Club. After the war ended, one of the 44 Kings bought a pint of expensive and imported Seagram's V.O. Canadian whiskey that would become the property of the last survivor of the group. That pint is still under lock and key at the Tompkins Alumni Center at SDSU.

The former 7-0 Club and the hamburger shop were squeezed into that building constructed by

Fred Carlson and Gus Dixon of nearby Flandreau. Dixon and his partners, J. C. Chimbouris and George Angelsen, leased the lot from the Madden family in 1932. Work started on their building on

The south half of the Nick's Hamburger Shop was the 7-0 Club during the 1940s. The bar had standing room at the bar and raised seating behind it along the bar's north wall. The blackboard behind the happy State College students carries the standings for the 7-0 Club Kittenball League. That's Gene Waltz, who later operated Waltz Hardware in Brookings, second from right.

August 5 of that year. It was to briefly become the Lincoln Café, which was opened with little fanfare on Saturday, September 24, 1932. Chimbouris moved to Brookings from Sioux Falls to operate the new café.

A newspaper account of the new business reported it used an oil burning stove installed by Thomas Norby of Brookings. Perhaps the unappetizing distillate oil exhaust from that stove was one reason the café never caught on. After a few months, it closed. To increase rental possibilities and income, the owners put a wall down the center of the already-tiny structure, and Gladys and Harold Niklason rented the north half. A few years later, in 1935, they purchased the entire building for $2,000, and two years later they purchased the lot from the Madden family for $10,000.

Incidentally, so unique is the building and the hamburger shop that in 1980 the structure was added to the National Register of Historic Places.

During the difficult years of the 1930s, most farm families in the area came to Brookings each Saturday to buy supplies, sell their milk and eggs, and catch up on the latest gossip and news. This Saturday night tradition continued up to the 1940s, and during those decades, Nick's Hamburger Shop became a popular eating place. Harold Jr. remembered that on those busy Saturdays he and his parents often served between 3,000 and 3,200 Nickburgers.

From the beginning the Niklasons were determined to serve quality food at the lowest price possible. Fresh hamburger buns (dinner rolls to begin with) were ordered each evening before closing to be delivered to the shop early the next day from a downtown bakery, sometimes from the City Bakery, or perhaps the Sweetheart Bakery,

Julian's Bakery, or Halsteads. To insure that only quality beef went into their burgers, Harold and Gladys eventually owned their own feedlot, raising the beef and supervising the butchering.

From their small herd, an average of three steers were butchered every twelve to fourteen days. When for some reason or another the herd numbers were not sufficient to handle demand, the Niklasons purchased hamburger from Sam and Gladys Artz, owners of the Artz Locker Plant at 307 Third Street, now the home of Hagman's Bakery. In an interview for the newspaper some years ago, Dexter Artz estimated that over a ten-year period, they sold over 200,000 pounds of hamburger to the Niklasons.

The same year that the Niklasons moved their shop to one of the best street corners in downtown Brookings, Prohibition ended and the South Dakota Legislature approved a law allowing for the sale of 3.2 beer. Within weeks the Brookings City Council was inundated with applications for the ten licenses the law allowed the city.

Among the license applicants, as published in the August 15, 1933, issue of the *Brookings Register*, was "Gladys Niklason, hamburger shop." It is interesting that Gladys signed the application as she was the one who decided the shop should be in Brookings because of what she assumed was a more imbibing population in Madison. Despite

Gladys and Harold Niklason behind their shop's counter amidst flowers sent by friends and well wishers on their 25th wedding anniversary. Note the sign on the wall: "Ice Cream, 10 and 15 cents, sundaes, 25 cents, and malts, 30 cents."

her aversion to liquor, the Niklasons were one of the ten successful applicants for a license.

They started selling beer along with their special Folgers coffee, hamburgers, and home-made pie. But they soon observed that with beer sales, many parents were reluctant to stop in with their children. Remember, in those days, women seldom if ever frequented the saloons and bars. If they imbibed at all, it was at private parties or in their own homes. The bars and watering holes were pretty much reserved for men. In 1936 Gladys and Harold decided to discontinue tap beer sales. However, they did continue to sell bottled beer until 1941.

Although customers found the hamburgers to their liking, they also became fans of the condiments, which included thin slices of onions, dill pickles, catsup, and a special Nickburger relish. That relish was and still is a particular favorite, the recipe for which was a closely held family secret for years. Eventually, the method of making the relish slipped out and was published in a column by John Beatty, who wrote a popular weekly column in the *Brookings Register.*

Harold and his son had a knack for carrying on friendly banter with customers as they worked the fry tank, which is not to say that they couldn't be a bit cranky toward an unruly customer from time to time. They carried on conversations with several customers at the same time without missing a beat or an order. They knew by name just about every one of their regular customers.

Harold and Gladys and son Harold Jr. had stock answers for many of the most often asked questions. Of course, people were always asking them the secret of their delicious hamburgers. They would confess that while it was a closely guarded family secret, they could say that considerable horse and rabbit meat went into the burgers. Then they would add that the ratio would be either half a horse and one rabbit or one horse and one rabbit, depending on the available supply that week. They'd chuckle and return to the bubbling caldron of simmering beef hamburger balls that needed squashing. To the question of what kinds of ice cream they served, they would brag about the three choices customers had: "white, plain, or vanilla."

While endeavoring to sell their hamburgers at the lowest possible price, the natural effects of inflation over time have dictated increases from the original five cents. The prices charged since the first day of operation in 1929 ranged from a nickel to more than a dollar:

1929-1941, 5 cents

1942-1950, 10 cents

1951-1962, 12 cents

1963-1968, 15 cents

1969-1970, 18 cents

1971-1975, 35 cents

1976-1978, 54 cents

1979-1980, 60 cents

1981-1988, 80 cents

1989-2000, 85 cents

2001-2004, 99 cents

2004- , $1.18

While the rule had always been to avoid the temptations to add to the shop's menu, when Harold Niklason Jr. assumed proud ownership during that record-setting year of 1947, he decided to add another choice. The hot dog, which could be prepared even faster than the hamburger, made its debut in the shop on Hobo Day 1947, intended for those customers eager to eat and run to other Hobo Day events. The experiment was a flop. While the shop turned out 4,500 hamburgers that busy day, only about twenty-four hot dogs were sold. The vote was overwhelming and the hot dog was dropped like a hot potato.

The corner location of the hamburger shop contributed to the success of the business, but its location near the city schools was also a factor. Long before the Niklasons came to town, citizens had decided to build the community's school a block from the business district. The first school in the 1880s was a two-story wood-frame affair at the corner of Fifth Avenue and Third Street that today is a small parking lot west of the Brookings Activities Center (formerly the Elks Club). Eventually, a larger brick school, called the Red Castle, was built on the grounds where today's old high school and Central Elementary School are located.

The Red Castle School served its purpose and was eventually razed. A new school, now called the "1921 Building," went up near where the beautiful old Red Castle once stood. The new school, and eventually Central Elementary School, were only a block away from the hamburger shop.

Especially before the school lunch system was started in Brookings in the early 1950s, students with loose change in their pockets flocked to Nick's for what they considered a well-rounded, inexpensive meal. Even after students were given a choice of school lunch food or lunching elsewhere, Nick's remained a popular stop for students between noon and 1 p.m. For just a quarter, students could enjoy two Nickburgers, a small bag of potato chips, a half-pint of milk, and a cookie. "About ten minutes before noon on school days we'd begin preparing about seven hundred hamburgers for the expected rush," remembered Harold Jr.

Aside from the gastronomical fare, part of the appeal of the hamburger shop is its décor and ambiance, or lack of it. Although there has been a recent major expansion, nothing changed for decades. The grill was originally placed facing east under the big display window. It was thought passersby would see the hamburger being cooked and be tempted to drop in. But the steam and vapors wafted from the cooking pan up onto the window, which had to be cleaned regularly. So in 1962, the cooking pan was moved to the south wall near where it remains today. A preparation and storage room was later added to the back of the shop, and the number of stools along the curving counter was increased from twelve to twenty.

In July 1975, Duane Larson, a local lad who had worked part-time as a waiter and dishwasher in the shop while in high school, purchased the shop from Harold Jr., who had decided to retire and tend to his horses. The new owner left everything almost exactly as he'd found it, with one major exception. The Coca Cola Company in the mid-1980s introduced a product they dubbed New Coke. It was a controversial change for Coca Cola, to be sure. Larson, a loyal fan of Coca Cola and a collector of Coke memorabilia, wasn't at all happy about the change. As a protest he discontinued carrying Coca Cola products in the shop. In fact, he literally threw Coke out the door. A photograph in the *Brookings Register* in 1985 shows Larson, seated on the curb in front of the shop, pouring a can of New Coke down the storm drain.

His disagreement and protest made the national news. *Newsweek* magazine on June 24, 1985, carried the story: "Saying 'No' to New Coke." In it, Larson is quoted as saying "they don't make Coke anymore." The story mentions that Larson had hung up a Pepsi Cola sign in his shop.

That national story wasn't the first time the little shop in Brookings, South Dakota, had gained national notoriety. The first time, however, the story had a more positive spin. In July 1978 the *Washington Post* newspaper published an article headlined "The Great American Hamburger Debate." The story listed the most popular hamburger shops in the nation as determined by a call-in poll by National Public Radio. Nick's Hamburger Shop was among the top eighty-two shops in the country. The *Post's* description of the nation's typical hamburger shop fit fairly well with the simple, far-from-ostentatious décor at Nick's.

Said the *Post* of the nation's best hamburger shops: "They are saturated with atmosphere and are usually very small and appear to be on their second generation of loyal customers. Their locations are almost always undistinguished in or near unattractive parking lots, busy intersections or down by the tracks. Their customers argue that no one needs a real plate and cloth napkins. Instead, you get the best hamburger in the world prepared before your eyes by some showman of a short-order clerk." Aside from Nick's location, which is arguably one of the two best intersections in Brookings, the description fits Nick's perfectly.

New owner Larson also made a few other changes of less controversy than removing Coca Cola products. He added cheeseburgers to the shop's limited menu. But many ardent Nickophiles took exception to adding cheese to a Nickburger. Some declared that purists simply did not order cheese on the sacrosanct hamburger. They

Duane Larson, at left, then a high school student working part time, would later purchase the shop from Harold Niklason Jr. That's Mary Williams serving a customer, and young Brookings businessman Bob Roe is second from right. Roe, now a stockbroker, later served as a school board member and a state representative of Brookings County.

assumed that only the younger, uninitiated customers and the first time out-of-towners would be so crass as to order Nickburgers garnished with cheese, wrote local columnist John Beatty.

Larson would operate the shop until the late summer of 2004 when he sold it to Dick Fergen, a graduate of Brookings High School and former student at SDSU. Fergen was one of those BHS kids who regularly made the quick run to Nick's for the twenty-five cent noon lunches. He's been eating Nickburgers since before he can remember.

He's is the son of Jim Fergen, a former SDSU basketball star who was in the men's clothing business in Brookings for many years before his death. In fact, his store was just a few doors south of where his oldest son, who played football and was the team co-captain his senior year, 1960, now works the shop's deep fry pan.

After a brief stint at South Dakota State University, Fergen left to find his future, which eventually led him back to Brookings and to the little shop at the corner of Main Avenue and Fifth Street. After buying the business, Fergen immediately established regular hours for the shop, including being open all day on Hobo Day. These changes, he said, had immediate results, bringing back longtime customers in droves.

Fergen also renewed the shop's long association with Coca Cola. Fergen put the shop on the Internet with its own website so fans the world over can check on what's new at Nick's (www.nickshamburgers.com). He sells t-shirts and sweatshirts with the shop's logo on them. He's working on a plan to market the famous home-made relish he makes following the old Niklason recipe. And Fergen purchased the empty lot next to his shop. It is now a pocket park where passersby and diners can sit during the warmer months. He arranges for local musicians to perform in the park on summer evenings, providing free entertainment for everyone.

But for the determination of Brookings firemen, the blaze on the cold night of March 3, 1985, might have consumed Nick's Hamburger Shop. It did destroy Ione's Café, the second story building next door (now the shop's pocket park), and a gift shop and Dr. Allen Westby's optometric shop. High winds that bitter cold night made the blaze difficult to battle.

While the park is now an asset to the hamburger shop, it was once the site of an old business building that burned in 1985 and nearly spelled the end for the shop. A fire broke out the night of March 3 in Ione's Café next door to Nick's. The café was destroyed, as were a gift shop and an optometric shop, but firemen worked throughout the cold night and saved the hamburger shop. Sadly, LeRoy VanderPol, 66, who roomed above the café, perished in the blaze.

It was in the spring of 2007 that Fergen decided to expand the shop into the south side of the building, with the eventual long-range possibility, depending upon city approval, of a drive-up window. For now, however, he's planning to just add a few more feet of counter space, a few more stools, and possibly another deep fry tank because of the increased business the shop's lone cooking pan has been hard pressed to keep up with during the busy times of the day.

Fergen is also considering having a mobile cooking unit made to be sent with cooks to

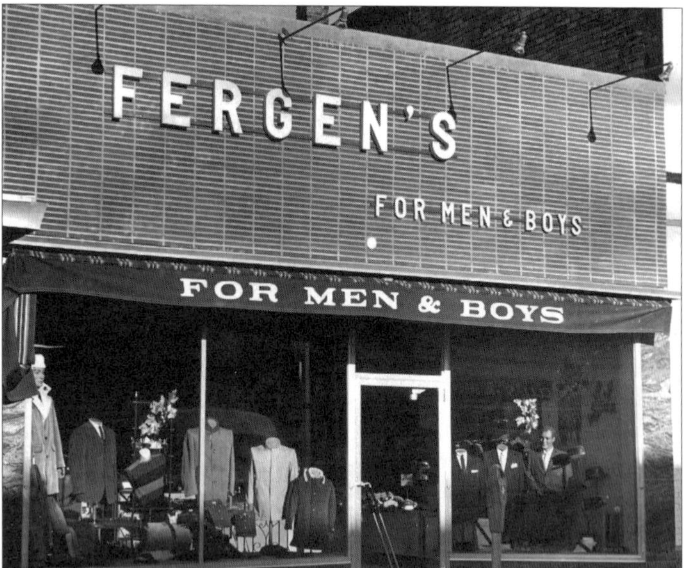

The Fergen family and Brookings businesses seem to go hand-in-hand. Current Nick's owner Dick Fergen's father, the late Jim Fergen, was proprietor of Fergen's store for men just a few blocks south of the hamburger shop, and Dick's younger brother Mike Fergen is owner of the famed Ray's Corner a block south on Main.

picnics and parties, offering the same delicious Nickburgers now confined to the shop. Fergen thinks that perhaps one day he may also develop a procedure that will allow him to prepare and ship frozen Nickburgers to customers around the world.

He's an enthusiastic entrepreneur who works long and hard to spread the Nickburger word. And he's there for the long haul, to continue the grand tradition of one of America's unique

Nick's Hamburger Shop and owner Dick Fergen's refurbished, bright red company truck.

hamburger shops on a busy corner in downtown Brookings.

Interestingly, the other desirable location in the Brookings business district is a block south, at the corner of Main Avenue and Fourth Street, where the present owner's younger brother, Mike Fergen, owns the very popular Ray's, a local watering hole and gathering spot.

Personable Jerry DeBlonk, a popular history teacher at Sioux Valley High School in the nearby community of Volga, is perhaps the world's leading authority on the hamburger shop and a devout Nickophile. DeBlonk has researched and written about the shop, and his work was valuable in the preparation of this little epistle. DeBlonk fondly remembers a 1985 visit to this area by friends from Ohio who had grown up in Brooklyn, New York. It was their first trip to South Dakota. DeBlonk joked that their idea of roughing it was to stay at a Holiday Inn that didn't have a swimming pool.

One day the DeBlonks took their eastern friends for lunch at Nick's Hamburger Shop. The visitors were somewhat taken aback that the shop was without booths, and they wondered about the square, lightly-waxed tissue laid on the counter in front of them. While waiting for their order to be filled, DeBlonk introduced them to some of the people seated nearby. As it happened, sitting next to DeBlonk's guest was well-known Brookings attorney, the late George S. Mickelson, who was enjoying a few Nickburgers for lunch. DeBlonk explained to his Ohio friends that George at the time was a candidate for governor of the state. DeBlonk remembers that the former Brooklynites were impressed. He said he believes that after that introduction, the quality of the small hamburger shop improved markedly in the eyes of the visiting Buckeyes. If the shop was good enough for a well-known VIP, it was good enough for them.

Over the years, stories about the lengths people would go to eat a Nickburger have been common. It may not happen every day, but it has often occurred that an alumnus of South Dakota State University or a former Brookings area resident takes great pains and some added expense to come back to Brookings to enjoy a serving at Nick's. One university graduate who lived in Thousand Oaks, California, cancelled his nonstop, coast-to-coast flight and elected to fly into Sioux Falls, rent a car, and drive to Brookings for a stop at Nick's before resuming his flight east. He ate eleven Nickburgers during his brief Brookings detour.

This writer was in the shop at about 11:30 a.m. in the winter of 2007 when an employee of a Sioux Falls firm drove to Brookings before lunch, ordered thirty-five Nickburgers to go, and took them back to Sioux Falls and his waiting co-workers.

A pilot on a North Central Airline's Minneapolis to Pierre flight with a stop in Brookings arranged to have his parents, who were Brookings

From 11 a.m. to about 2 p.m. the crew at Nick's Hamburger Shop is busy filling orders and dodging one another in the little shop's crowded work space. Nearly a thousand hamburgers might be sold during the lunch period.

Customers park on the stools and stand along the wall awaiting their orders of Nickburgers.

residents, pick up a sack of Nickburgers and meet his plane when it landed. The sack was handed up to the cockpit, and the happy pilot enjoyed his lunch on the flight from Brookings to Pierre.

Then there is the story of the resident of the tiny town of Astoria in Duel County north and east of Brookings. He was flying from Los Angeles to Chicago. For some reason, his flight was held up for nine hours in Omaha. To while away the time, the man boarded another flight to Sioux Falls, rented a car there, and drove to Brookings for a brief stop at Nick's Hamburger Shop. He ate nine Nickburgers in all, then retraced his steps and worked his way by car and plane back to Omaha to resume his original Chicago flight.

Ruth Fay, a fan of Nickburgers, wrote in December 1999 that when she was a graduate student at South Dakota State University from 1966 to 1968, she owned a Great Dane dog named

Baron. "As far as I know, Baron was the only dog Nick [Harold Jr.] allowed in his hamburger shop," she said. "My former husband would take Baron to Nick's and Baron would sit across from the counter along the wall. Nick from time to time would flip Baron a hamburger and Baron would catch it in mid-air." The dog became so fond of

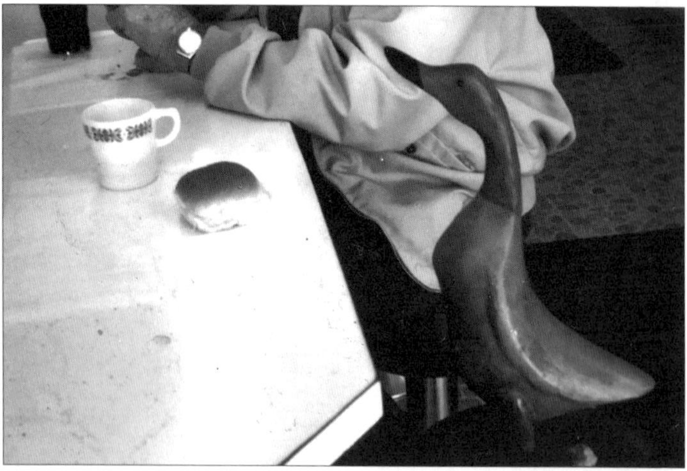

A dog named Baron occasionally begged a burger at Nick's, and from time to time a pig might over-consume Nickburgers at one sitting, but only one duck has ever been served: a carved one that a customer enjoyed photographing in unusual settings around the world.

Nickburgers that whenever he was near the shop he would "paint" the shop with his nose and wag his tail expectantly.

When former SDSU student, Vietnam jet pilot, and Medal of Honor winner Leo Thorsness was in Brookings for the unveiling of a plaque in his honor at the university's Memorial Grove, he and his wife made a point to stop at Nick's for a quick treat before returning to Sioux Falls for their flight home to Arizona.

The late Bernard Guss of Brookings wrote in 1991: "My fondest memory of Nick's was when I was ten or eleven. We were strapped for funds as my father had passed away when I was younger. My birthday request to my mother was that I be allowed to eat as many Nick's hamburgers as I could at one sitting. It played havoc with the family's cash flow problems, but I sure put away a lot of those ten cent burgers."

The ten Nickburgers Guss ate may have been a record for a ten-year-old, but stakes were raised in 2006 and 2007. On Sept. 22, 2006, Brian Kral of Sleepy Eye, Minnesota, stopped by the shop after classes at SDSU to celebrate his twenty-third birthday. On the spur of the moment he decided to try for a new Nickburger record: twenty-three burgers.

Until Kral dropped in, the shop's record stood at a healthy twenty-two, set six months before Kral's valiant effort. On Feb. 18, 2006, a 21-year-old Mormon missionary, Elder Bill Bond, was in Brookings as part of his schooling.

He downed the hamburgers at a pace of about one every three minutes, completing his feast in seventy minutes. His reward was a Nickburger sweatshirt and his humongous meal at no charge. But he turned down the free piece of pie offered him by waitress Laurie Austin. "I could probably eat it," he told her, "but I think I best not."

Then along came the 6' 3", 250-pound Kral, an engineering major at SDSU who was also working at Daktronics. His record was witnessed by his buddy Collin Kessler. Owner Dick Fergen awarded Kral his prize t-shirt and then ceremoni-

SDSU student Brian Kral set a Nick's Hamburger eating record on Sept. 22, 2006. The engineering student from Sleepy Eye, MN, downed twenty-three burgers. Owner Dick Fergen and waitress Neva Bullivant, at right, verified the record. A Nick's t-shirt and no bill for the burgers were his prizes.

ously tore up the bill for the twenty-three burgers.

The record fell again in February 2007 when local Nickburger connoisseur Terry Nicolai dropped in to give the record a go. He chomped down twenty-four burgers, faltering slightly only on burger number twenty-three but setting the new mark at one sitting. After he'd had a few minutes to recover, he allowed as how the effort wasn't that bad, and figured he'd come back in a few weeks and go for a new mark. But the rules of the eating game at Nick's say that if a record is broken, the champion must wait until someone else ups that record number of burgers before the newly-deposed champion can try again.

Fergen is settling in to a new, larger hamburger shop, having expanded into the south half of the building in the summer of 2007. The space for expansion through the years has, as mentioned earlier, served many businesses. Clair D. Husby remembered when the south half of the building was the office for an insurance agency—Steen's Insurance—owned by Conway Steen.

Husby remembers one particular window display in the insurance office. It was hardly conducive to hamburger sales. The display featured photographs in living color of gruesome automobile accidents. "I remember having to walk by those photographs and at the same time take in the aroma of Nick's, and it created a very uncomfortable feeling, to say the least."

Hal Lynn of Claremont, California, was a member of the Brookings High School football, basketball, and track teams from 1942 to 1945. He has fond memories of the hamburger shop. "When we returned home from road trips we were each given fifteen cents by the coach. The entire team would go down to Nick's for hamburgers and a soft drink," he said. "For many of us this was significant as we had little money for eating out."

Waldo E. Johnson of Niceville, Florida, a 1940 graduate of Brookings High School, was also a member of the famous 44 Kings mentioned

Many customers still remember waitress Mary Williams, here tending the cooking pot.

earlier. He and the other ROTC cadets all remembered the 7-0 Club next door and, of course, Nick's. Johnson was mentioned in a column in the *Brookings Register* that included letters and comments from local servicemen away from home and fighting in WW II.

It seems that in nearly every letter home from the theaters of war, the writers mentioned how much he or she missed Nick's hamburgers. It seemed the burgers ranked right up there with Mom's apple pie. One of the men fighting in the South Pacific, Lorys Larson of Brookings, was quoted in an issue of the *Pacific Stars and Stripes.* Larson told a *Stars and Stripes* reporter that he was looking forward to getting back to Brookings and having a Nick's hamburger.

Lorys did return to Brookings and enjoyed Nickburgers for the rest of his life. He became a professor in the College of Engineering at SDSU, and his son, Duane, became the third owner of the hamburger shop when he purchased it from Harold Niklason Jr. in 1975.

Now, the spatula has been passed to Dick Fergen, and he's working hard to keep the Nick-burger tradition alive.

This old photograph of Brookings' Main Avenue in the 1920s shows the Montgomery-Ward building at right. The first store visible at left is the Red Owl Grocery Store.

Brookings' Main Avenue looked like this when the Nick's Hamburger Shop opened in 1929. This picture looks to the north. The Masonic Hall is at left, still wearing its steeple. Across the street is the Montgomery-Ward Building.

Looking north down Main Avenue the year that Gladys and Harold Niklason located their Nick's Hamburger Shop in Brookings.